W9-API-256

Teen Guide to SIDE GIGS

Working in the New Economy

Stuart A. Kallen

San Diego, CA

About the Author

Stuart A. Kallen is the author of more than 350 nonfiction books for children and young adults. He has written on topics ranging from the theory of relativity to the art of electronic dance music. In 2018, Kallen won a Green Earth Book Award from the Nature Generation environmental organization for his book *Trashing the Planet: Examining the Global Garbage Glut*. In his spare time, he is a singer, songwriter, and guitarist in San Diego, California.

For more information, contact:
ReferencePoint Press, Inc.
PO Box 27779
San Diego, CA 92198
www.ReferencePointPress.com

LIBRARY OF CONGRESS CATALOGING-IN-PUBLICATION DATA

Names: Kallen, Stuart A., 1955- author.
Title: Teen guide to side gigs : working in the new economy / by Stuart A. Kallen.
Description: San Diego, CA : ReferencePoint Press, Inc., 2022. | Includes bibliographical references and index.
Identifiers: LCCN 2021039371 (print) | LCCN 2021039372 (ebook) | ISBN 9781678202422 (library binding) | ISBN 9781678202439 (ebook)
Subjects: LCSH: Teenagers--Vocational guidance--Juvenile literature. | Gig economy--Juvenile literature. | Temporary employment--Juvenile literature.
Classification: LCC HF5381.2 .K349 2022 (print) | LCC HF5381.2 (ebook) | DDC 331.702--dc23
LC record available at https://lccn.loc.gov/2021039371
LC ebook record available at https://lccn.loc.gov/2021039372

Contents

Introduction   **4**
The Growing Side-Gig Economy

Chapter One   **9**
Little Experience Required

Chapter Two   **16**
Focus on Food

Chapter Three   **23**
Art and Design

Chapter Four   **30**
Writing and Translating

Chapter Five   **37**
Music and Video

Chapter Six   **44**
Making Instructional Videos

Chapter Seven   **50**
Technology and Programming

Source Notes   56
Other Side Gigs Worth Exploring   59
Find Out More   60
Index   62
Picture Credits   64

The Growing Side-Gig Economy

When the COVID-19 pandemic hit in March 2020, Samantha Sands lost her public relations (PR) job in San Diego, California. As the bills piled up, Sands (who was twenty-five at the time) continued to work with a few PR clients who still needed her services during the pandemic. When money from PR work slowed to a trickle, Sands got creative and started a side gig. Also known as a side hustle, side gigs are any type of moneymaking work performed outside of a regular job. And side hustlers work for themselves, unlike temporary or part-time workers, who work for others.

Sands launched her side gig by drawing on her previous experience as a bridal consultant during her college years: "It was a fun job with good commission if I did well,"[1] she explains. While many people were canceling their weddings during the pandemic, Sands found that some were thinking about holding virtual weddings online or making plans to tie the knot when the crisis ended. Sands advertised her wedding planning skills on social media sites like Facebook and Pinterest. Instead of bemoaning the pandemic, she put a positive spin on the concept of holding intimate, low-stress, outdoor weddings. Sands says her side gig as a wedding consultant brought in an extra $1,200 a month. In an October 2020 interview, she notes: "I use it to pay some bills, but I also use it as a cushion. . . . We don't know what the future holds, and I would rather be safe than struggling."[2]

Working in the Gig Economy

Even before the pandemic, a growing number of people were working short-term jobs with flexible hours that paid by the gig. And as unemployment soared in 2020, many more joined this so-called gig economy. According to the Freelancers Union, which advocates for independent workers, 57 million Americans worked in the gig economy in 2019. Around 2 million more started their own side gigs in 2020; many of these had never been self-employed before.

Even after people started going back to work in 2021 side hustles remained a way of life for many. According to a survey by the Jobvite employee recruiting company, 53 percent of American workers in 2021 said they had a side gig or intended to get one soon. A year earlier, that number was only 36 percent.

As the Jobvite figures show, a new spirit of entrepreneurship emerged during the pandemic. Laid-off restaurant workers became personal chefs and caterers, unemployed hair stylists set up shops in their homes, and gym instructors began training clients in parks, basements, and backyards. As economist Steven Hamilton explains, "As horrible as [the pandemic was], and as badly as it has affected so many people, it has pushed people to come up with new ideas and products and services."[3] This change is reflected in the growing number of websites that connect freelancers to customers. The arts and crafts website Etsy noted that its revenue nearly doubled in 2020 as artisans expanded their product lines to meet demand. And the freelancer site Fiverr International reported that the number of new freelancers registering on its site rose nearly 50 percent during the pandemic.

Launching New Businesses

While some individual endeavors turn into full-time businesses, many people work side gigs to earn money while they are in school or between jobs. This type of independent work is especially appealing to the first wave of young professionals in Generation Z, who are currently entering the workforce. According to a 2020 survey by Girls With Impact, which helps young women launch their own businesses, 53 percent of Gen Z men and women expect to run their own businesses one day.

For many, the path to running a business begins with a side gig. Social media sites like Instagram and TikTok are brimming with videos by Gen Z folks who explain how they are earning money through side gigs. While driving and delivery are the most common side gigs, many are discovering ways to make money using their hobbies, education, and creative talents. Those with literary talents are writing ad copy, editing books and articles, and translating documents. People who possess information technology (IT) skills are building websites, helping others set up online businesses, and developing apps and games. The artistic are customizing clothes, writing songs, making jewelry, and selling paintings and photographs. With so many side gig opportunities available to them, journalist Kian Bakhtiari refers to Gen Z as "Generation Side Hustle."[4]

Twenty-five-year-old singer-songwriter Alissa Musto put her creative talents to work when she lost her job as a cruise ship musician during the pandemic. Musto launched a successful side gig by filming piano lessons for a music-teaching app. She also began posting music videos on Instagram in an effort to become an influencer. Musto cites the benefits of working side gigs: "I feel like I am still being moderately productive and working on my brand rather than just sitting around waiting for my industry to resume. . . . And having these side gigs has helped me tremendously mentally during the pandemic because it has given me a way to exercise my brain and contribute."[5]

Taxes and Regulations

There are downsides to the gig economy. While side gigs often allow workers to set their own hours and keep all of the money they earn, there are other issues to consider. Those who work for

Growing Interest in Side Gigs

By 2020 one out of every three Americans had some sort of side gig—and more were looking to start new side gigs in 2021. Those findings come from a December 2020 survey conducted by the Harris Poll for the workplace online platform provider Zapier. When asked how long ago they had started their side gigs, 67 percent said they had done so within the past three years and 31 percent said they got started in 2020.

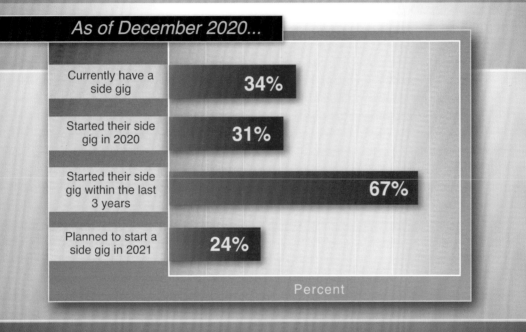

As of December 2020...

	Percent
Currently have a side gig	34%
Started their side gig in 2020	31%
Started their side gig within the last 3 years	67%
Planned to start a side gig in 2021	24%

themselves are responsible for providing their own health insurance. They must also pay taxes, including Social Security and Medicare on their total earnings; however, self-employed workers can lower their tax bills by deducting business-related expenses. These expenses include costs related to using a personal vehicle, advertising, supplies, and maintaining a home office. To deduct expenses, the self-employed are required to keep good financial records and save all receipts related to their business expenses. Tax experts recommend that the self-employed set aside about one-third of their earnings in a savings account to pay taxes when they are due.

Those who work side gigs must also adhere to health and safety regulations. Occupational licenses are required for those who handle food, care for children, style hair, and engage in other professions. And many municipalities require the self-employed to purchase an annual business license.

Individuals who earn money doing side gigs get no paid vacations, workers' comp, sick leave, or other benefits generally provided by employers. Despite these drawbacks, side gigs allow you to take control of your life and be your own boss. Side gigs aren't necessarily a route to becoming a millionaire, but who knows where they can lead?

Chapter One

Little Experience Required

Side Gig Stats

42 percent of those with side hustles are optimistic about the future of their gigs.

DollarSprout, "Side Hustle Report," July 22, 2021. https://dollarsprout.com.

Anyone hoping to launch a side gig can find plenty of information on the internet. Countless articles and videos have been posted with a breathtaking array of moneymaking side hustles that can be done by those going to school, working part-time, or even hoping to launch a new business. Many gigs require specific skills. Side-gig websites like Fiverr offer work to people with experience in design, marketing, writing, programming, and business. Anyone entering this job market is facing stiff competition; yet there is no reason for side-gig newbies who lack training or specialized skills to be discouraged. There are a number of side hustles that require little previous experience, especially for those who do not mind working hard and getting their hands dirty. These hustles range from making deliveries to walking dogs to washing cars. What they have in common is that they can be started quickly and learned on the job. And like all side gigs, the workers are in control: They decide how often to work, when to work, and how hard to work.

Making Deliveries

About 40 percent of Americans stopped going to their jobs every day when the COVID-19 pandemic shut down businesses across the country in 2020. And the restrictions enacted to slow the spread of the disease changed people's eating and shopping habits practically overnight. Suddenly millions of people were ordering nearly everything online, from clothing and toiletries to groceries and restaurant meals. All of these items were delivered by an army of drivers. Many of these dashing drivers and hustling bikers were making deliveries for the first time. By the time the lockdowns ended, people had grown used to the convenience of having food and goods dropped off at their door, and delivery drivers remained in high demand.

In Beaverton, Oregon, a college student with the online name of Black Sugar Ice Jelly was one of those new delivery workers who had had little previous experience. In 2020 Black Sugar Ice Jelly was a Dasher, someone who worked part-time for Door-Dash, a company that provides home delivery services to local restaurants. He notes, "The pay was not bad. . . . It's probably one of the most flexible jobs of all time; you dash for a couple hours or several here and there, and you don't if you don't want to."[6]

DoorDash says its drivers average $18 an hour and get to keep 100 percent of their tips. The company is one of many, including GrubHub, Postmates, Instacart, and Uber Eats, that provide flexible side gigs to grocery and restaurant delivery drivers. Those who are not interested in food delivery can work as a UPS Personal Vehicle Driver, using their own cars to deliver packages.

As a side gig, there are definite benefits to working for delivery platforms. Drivers can pick shifts whenever they wish to work, and they are paid on a weekly basis. There are some basic requirements, however. Workers must pass a criminal background check, and companies usually require their workers to be at least eighteen years old and have a valid driver's license and car insurance.

Some food delivery services do not require driver's licenses: in large cities, workers are allowed to use bicycles, scooters, or even go on foot. Those who work in cold, rainy climates may prefer to make deliveries in a car or truck. Andres Hernandez was riding his electric bike 50 miles (80.4km) a day as a Dasher in Queens, New York. "It's hard," says Hernandez. "Especially when it's raining and snowing."[7]

While using a personal vehicle to make deliveries is easier than traveling by bike, the cost of gasoline, repairs, and insurance cuts into a driver's profits. Drivers are also responsible for parking fees, tolls, and traffic tickets. These costs can really have a negative effect on earnings. According to a study by the side-hustle website Financial Wolves, Dashers can make anywhere between $18.50 an hour before expenses and earn as little as $1.45 after expenses are subtracted. This vast difference depends on variables such as distances between deliveries, low demand for deliveries, weather, and other issues. But as Chicago Dasher Choncé Maddox writes: "If you have a goal you'd like to reach where having extra money would help, it's quick and easy to get signed up and give it a try. Set an income goal, determine when you can drive, and then see how much you can earn."[8]

For Pet Lovers

Professional dog walkers are easy to spot on the street. They often command a collection of big and small dogs leashed together in a mass of fur and wagging tails. It might look easy—and sometimes it is, but not always. Dog walkers, who are responsible for safely handling pets that are beloved by their owners, have to deal with dogs that bark, bite, or lunge at strangers or other dogs. And dog walkers must pick up and dispose of piles of dog poop. For doing this, dog walkers can earn as much as $28 an hour with an average hourly wage of nearly $15, according to the salary data site PayScale. The difference is based on where the dog walker lives. Dog-walking wages are significantly higher in affluent neighborhoods in big cities, whereas the pay in small towns is usually much lower.

Dog walkers need to be able to handle at least three dogs at a time. And walkers need to invest in leashes, dog harnesses of various sizes, leash clips, poop scoopers and bags, and other equipment. Most dog walkers find customers among friends and family members, but many turn to apps that help them attract new clients. Platforms like Wag and Rover work much like delivery apps. Prospective dog walkers sign up with the

Besides loving dogs, professional dog walkers need to have some knowledge about dog behavior. It also helps to have a healthy dose of patience and some basic equipment, including leashes, poop scoops, and bags.

app and submit to a background check. They choose a schedule and pick the type of pet they wish to care for. Walkers get paid in two to seven days. A Wag dog walker who goes by the screen name LynneP1978 describes her side gig like this: "In two months I've walked 120 dogs and made $2500. I average $350 per week. . . . I work full-time as an executive assistant at my other job . . . so [I] do most of my walking all day Saturday–Monday (I like to do 5–7 dogs a day). . . . I'm a busy girl but love it!!! Keep in mind I also live and work in very affluent, populated areas in West Los Angeles where there are a ton of dogs and owners who will spare no expense."[9]

It is relatively easy to get started with a dog-walking side gig. Other side gigs involving pets require more knowledge, preparation, and commitment. Doggy day care and pet boarding services are two of these. Some pet owners are willing to pay what is essentially a short-term babysitter to care for their pet while they are at work. And when people go on vacation, they often seek a place to board their pets so that they are not home alone. In both cases, the caregiver has to have some experience working with animals. Those who take other people's pets into their homes must understand how to deal with nervous or frightened animals that find themselves in unfamiliar surroundings.

Washing and Detailing Vehicles

Starting a car-washing and detailing business is as easy as picking out a catchy name for the enterprise and advertising on local social networking services like Nextdoor.com. You can also print up flyers or business cards and leave them on community bulletin boards at grocery stores and laundromats. While waiting for customers to contact you, put together a menu featuring prices for basic services like external washing, waxing, interior vacuuming, polishing, trim cleaning, and tire cleaning. To get an idea of the going rate in your area, check out the service menu of competitors. A blogger named Baxter, who runs the Carwash Country website, also recommends buying T-shirts, caps, and service uniforms featuring your business name. In addition to being good advertising, Baxter says a good, clean, basic uniform reassures customers that you can be trusted with their expensive vehicles: "In the world of detailing, appearance is everything. . . . While the job you do is what really matters, a professional appearance (including the clothing you wear) can win over customers in the market for detailing services."[10]

Startup costs for a car-detailing gig are minimal; beginners can start with a package of good microfiber towels, car wash soap and wax, a few buckets and sponges, and detailing brushes and polish. Those who wish to invest more can purchase a garden hose and an electric pressure washer. In places where there are large apartment buildings and no water or electricity is available, a detailer might need to purchase a portable power generator and small water tank. And, of course, those who offer mobile car-cleaning services need their own vehicles to transport themselves and their equipment to gigs.

Small business experts recommend that individuals who wash and detail cars, like all side hustlers, consult with a tax accountant when it comes time to file income taxes in April. Accountants will want to see a profit-and-loss spreadsheet that shows money spent on your gig and payments received for your work. The cost of supplies, advertising, and car mileage incurred driving to and from gigs may be deductible expenses, meaning they could be used to lower the amount of income on which you pay taxes.

Anyone who runs a side gig like car washing, doggy day care, or delivery will tell you that their hustles require them to think creatively, work hard, and never rest on past success. While it might be easier to take a regular job and let someone else worry about the hassles, side hustles can be more satisfying. You learn marketable skills, which builds confidence. And when the work is done, the profits are yours and yours alone.

Q&A Interview: Delivery Side Gig

Carol Cote works in the real estate business in San Diego, California. She has been working a side gig as a UPS Personal Vehicle Driver since 2020.

Q: How would you describe your side gig?

A: I am a part-time delivery driver who uses her own car to make deliveries during the holidays and other busy periods.

Q: How did you get into this side gig?

A: A friend told me about it, and I applied. During the pandemic when the number of people ordering online skyrocketed, UPS was very eager to hire self-employed drivers.

Q: What are the requirements for this gig?

A: You have to be at least 21 years old and be able to lift and carry packages up to 70 pounds. You need a valid driver's license, car insurance, and be able to show that you have had no accidents that were your fault in the past 3 years. And your car can have no political bumper stickers or company logos.

Q: Can you describe your typical workday?

A: I load packages into my car and deliver them to residences. I input information into a tracking device regarding each package delivery, along with my time and car mileage. The tracking device helps plan the most efficient route for deliveries.

Q: What do you like most about this side gig?

A: I like the flexibility of working a side gig, and the pay is pretty good. I enjoy working on my own and being outside, and I like the physical aspect of it (I lost weight with this gig). People are very appreciative, too, for the delivery drivers. One time I even delivered a little boy's birthday cake, and he was very excited to see me.

Q: What do you like least about this side gig?

A: When I don't have enough hours because there is a surplus of drivers. Also it is sometimes hard to lug big packages up a lot of stairs. And badly designed apartment complexes make the job difficult—sometimes it is very hard to figure out where individual units are located. [And] I often have to waste time referring to maps to find the right address.

Q: What personal qualities are most valuable for this type of side gig?

A: I think a good work ethic is valuable. You have to be able to work independently and really hustle. Being good at problem solving is important. And you need to have an attention to detail so that packages don't get delivered to the wrong place.

Q: What advice do you have for someone who might be interested in doing something similar?

A: If you like being physically active instead of being in an office all day, this is a good gig. But I could see it being physically wearing in the long term unless you are relatively healthy. Also the company has certain expectations about how many packages were to be delivered in a certain time frame. So you have to be focused and on top of your game.

Chapter Two

Focus on Food

Side Gig Stats

30 percent of side hustlers say they perform their gigs just to make ends meet, while 60 percent save the money or spend it on extras like recreation and entertainment.

Amanda Dixon, "Survey: Nearly 1 in 3 Side Hustlers Needs the Income to Stay Afloat," Bankrate, June 5, 2019. www.bankrate.com.

In 2020 Thuy Pham was working at her dream job as a private hairstylist in Portland, Oregon. She made good money giving fancy haircuts to executives, touring pop stars, and other wealthy clients. When the pandemic lockdown hit, Pham was stuck at home with no job and little to do. Instead of binge-watching television or doom-scrolling on her phone, Pham searched YouTube for recipes that featured Vietnamese food. Pham, who was born in Vietnam and is vegan, had lots of experience cooking up meatless dishes for her friends and family. She began experimenting with her native cuisine, refashioning traditional meat-based dishes into vegetarian dishes like mock pork belly and vegan bao buns. As a way to stay in touch with the outside world, Pham livestreamed on Instagram as she cooked. "Within minutes of going live, I had customers asking to buy my pork belly slabs," Pham says. "I immediately thought that this could be a way for me to make ends meet until I could go back to work as a hairstylist."[11]

Pham shipped more than one hundred local orders within seven days of going live. She was sending her bao buns all over the country within two weeks. By 2021 Pham's mail order business was so good she was making plans to open a vegan Vietnamese deli in Portland. She had no plans to return to her old job.

Foodie Freelancers

Pham was one of countless unemployed Americans who started their own food business during the pandemic. And small business experts say the home-based cooking trend will continue to grow since food-related side gigs offer the promise of high profits with low startup costs. Those with extra time on their hands are marketing homemade bread, gourmet meals, and homemade hot sauce. While some are laid off chefs, line cooks, and caterers, others—like Pham—are experienced foodies doing what they love most. Many turned to apps such as DishDivvy, Shef, CozyMeal, and EatWith to market their meals to hungry customers.

DishDivvy, which is only available in California, is one of the most popular cook-to-customer apps. And during the pandemic, the site experienced an eightfold increase in the number of chefs offering meals. Cooks who register on the site must first be vetted, a process that can take several weeks. DishDivvy's Cook Support Team conducts in-person interviews with chefs, inspects their kitchens, and even tastes sample dishes. Chefs must also possess a California Food Handler Card. To obtain the card, applicants must learn about food safety and pass an online test. Other apps, such as Shef, which operates in New York City, Chicago, Houston, Boston, and Seattle, require city or state food handling certificates in these areas.

Wherever cooks are located, the apps work the same way. Cooks provide their home address and determine what kinds of meals they wish to make. They create menus and set prices. The cooking apps take 15 percent of a meal's cost and charge each customer an extra dollar per order. DishDivvy says cooks using the service made an average monthly income of $2,500 in 2020.

Marketing Food Online

While cooking apps make it easier to connect with customers, they are not always necessary. Dan Palmer's side hustle began when he decided to cook some meals for a friend after she had a baby. He delivered several frozen ready-to-eat meals to the new mom—as a gift. The woman, who works full-time and has three kids, loved the meals and offered to pay Palmer $100 for five dishes per week. About half the money covers the cost of the ingredients; the rest is Palmer's to keep. He ends up earning about $10 an hour for cooking up pasta dishes, casseroles, and Asian- and Mexican-style dishes. He freezes the meals so they keep all week. Palmer, who works this side gig with his wife, explains: "This cooking side hustle really works out well for everyone. Our friend gets a home cooked meal every day of the (work) week, and we make some side money in the process. We also make the meals big enough for her family so that there's always leftovers for lunch the next day. . . . And whenever we make her a meal, we usually just make a double batch so that we have one for ourselves too with little additional effort!"[12]

Specialist Success

Ashlyn Balch is another cook who launched her food-based side hustle cooking for friends and family. Balch always loved fancy cookies. Her appreciation for these delectable morsels stems from childhood, when she used to help her grandmother with holiday baking. Balch, who was working as a clinical dietitian in Kansas City, Missouri, in 2020, took a cake-decorating class that inspired her to create a side gig called Sprinkled and Frosted: "I started practicing random cookie designs at home, and I would give them away to family and friends to get feedback. Then they started ordering from me. [The business] really started with my family and friends."[13]

As her business took off Balch learned to increase her profits by changing her buying habits. For instance, buying flour in bulk costs a lot less than buying a five-pound bag each week. She also tries to keep her designs fresh by exploring online sites for ideas. She explains, "I can see what I like, what I don't like, and how to pair different color schemes together."[14]

Many home bakers, including those who create decorative cakes, have turned their hobby into a money-making side gig. Most start small and spend a lot of time searching for new ideas and techniques.

Most side gigs, food related and otherwise, start small. Some stay small. Others blossom into full-scale businesses. Scott Zalkind's hobby-turned-side-gig is one of the latter. While working as a health care project manager, Zalkind, of Hayward, California, began making his own hot sauce. He named his creation Lucky Dog Hot Sauce, after his dog. "I've always loved spicy foods, since I was a little kid," he says. "My brother and I would always dare each other to eat hotter stuff."[15] After a while, Zalkind had so much extra homemade hot sauce he began giving away about twenty-five bottles every month to friends and business contacts. People liked his sauce so much that he started getting requests for it from chefs and owners of local grocery stores, wine shops, and other businesses.

The growing interest in Lucky Dog Hot Sauce soon outstripped Zalkind's ability to make enough. This led him to sign a contract with a food processer called Village Green Foods in Irvine, California. Village Green is in the business of cooking up soups, sauces, and spreads for large restaurant chains. The company also works with hundreds of side hustlers who pay them to produce small batches of tomato sauce, chili oil, gourmet cocktail mixes, and hot sauce. This allows small producers like Zalkind to get out of the kitchen so they can concentrate on selling their food products at farmers' markets, online, and elsewhere.

TikTok Food Stars

Zalkind has tattoos of hot peppers and sports a purple mohawk hairstyle (he trades hot sauce for haircuts). This unique look helped him stand out when he appeared on the popular YouTube series *Hot Ones*, where celebrities like the Jonas Brothers and Kumail Nanjiani are interviewed as they eat foods slathered with high-powered hot sauce. YouTube helped increase Zalkind's sales, but he is not the only one to benefit from video-sharing sites. Social media platforms and video-sharing sites like YouTube feature thousands of how-to cooking videos that have helped people launch their own cooking side hustles. When Eitan Bernath was growing up, he watched those videos and taught himself to cook. In 2021, nineteen-year-old Bernath was posting cooking videos on TikTok and had more than 1.6 million followers.

Like most TikTok stars, Bernath is charismatic, attractive, and photogenic. His video recipes, aimed at teenagers, are short, easy to make, and offer clear instructions. But Bernath's celebrity status would not have been possible without an explosion of interest in home-cooked meals during the pandemic. The hashtag #TikTokFood, known as FoodTok, amassed more than 25 billion views in 2020 and spawned a slew of new Gen Z cooking stars like Bernath. Most have zero experience working as a professional chef. As technology reporter Taylor Lorenz writes: "Many Gen Z stars on FoodTok. . . wonder why anyone would pay their dues at a grueling restaurant job when they could be building their own brand online."[16]

FoodTok also attracts restaurant professionals who were laid off during the pandemic and now have no intention of returning to their jobs. The most popular FoodTok foodies earn millions of dollars for a few hours' work every day. They earn money through advertising deals, sponsorships, and the TikTok creator fund, which pays video creators according to the number of hits a video attracts. Some enhance their income by starting their own brand of chocolate bars or cookies. Others are launching cookware lines or publishing cookbooks. While Bernath respects classically trained chefs and professional restaurateurs, he believes his generation is more attracted to do-it-yourselfers: "I think what TikTok has done with Gen Z and teaching people how to cook, it's just more relatable. The feedback I hear all the time is, 'If this 18-year-old Eitan can cook this so effortlessly, then I can, too.'"[17]

While Bernath has a point, only a small number of TikTok creators actually earn a living from the videos they make. Nevertheless, almost anyone can excel as a side hustler in the food business. All one needs is the willingness to work hard, study the market, and come up with a unique product that will singe their mouths, sweeten their moods, or satisfy their desire for a delicious meal.

Q&A Interview: A Cooking Side Gig

Teddy Charles is a real estate professional in San Diego, California. She has been cooking meals as a side gig since 2016.

Q: How would you describe your side gig?

A: I work as a personal chef whose clients suffer from a variety of auto-immune problems [that causes] inflammation of the joints, nerves, and digestive system. I provide them with organic, healthy meals based on the Paleo Auto-Immune (AIP) Diet.

Q: How did you get into this side gig?

A: I was asked to cook by one of my friends because she doesn't like cooking, but she knew that I did. She subsequently referred several other clients to me. I have been cooking for the same people once a week for at least four years, which shows how well it is working.

Q: Can you describe your typical workday?

A: I go shopping based on a list and a menu that I have pre-prepared, then cook the dishes in my home. Once I have finished, I deliver some of the food, or clients come and collect it.

Q: What do you like most about this side gig?

A: My specialty is creating new recipes and amending common recipes so that they fit with the AIP diet. This venture has really turned into a collaboration because I am constantly reviewing my clients' feedback, which helps me improve the dishes that I cook. Based on their feedback, I add new dishes so I have an increasing number to choose from every week. Sometimes I remove or adjust dishes that are not so favorable. It's important to have enough variety so that dishes are not repeated more than once every month or two months. It is also wonderful to feel that I am helping improve their health and well-being.

Q: What do you like least about this side gig?

A: It can be a little intense when I am running behind schedule because I'm always conscious of trying to keep costs down (I charge on an hourly basis). It can also be stressful when a dish doesn't come out exactly as planned although sometimes something that doesn't look good tastes good.

Q: What personal qualities do you find most valuable for this type of work?

A: Being creative and always coming up with new recipes; otherwise it would get boring for me as a cook and also for the clients.

Q: What advice do you have for teens who might be interested in doing something similar?

A: The great thing about what I do is that it's a real niche in the market. It's aimed at people who are eating a very specific and controlled diet. So finding a niche is important when it comes to separating yourself from the competition. I have generally found that a lot of people don't know how to cook. They also have limited knowledge about what foods to eat and what effects various foods have on the body. I suggest doing research and becoming knowledgeable in this area. I believe that cooking and meal planning is a good trend to get involved with since more people are recognizing the connection between a good diet and overall health.

Chapter Three

Art and Design

Side Gig Stats

41 percent of side hustlers say they started their business to spend more time doing what they enjoy.

Vistaprint, "STUDY: Millions of Americans Have a 'Side Hustle' to Boost Their Incomes and Pursue Their Passions," August 1, 2019. https://news.vistaprint.com.

Three-quarters of artists and designers work for themselves, according to a 2019 poll by Upwork titled "Freelancing in America Survey." Traditionally, these independent gig workers have struggled to make ends meet. But freelance employment platforms like Upwork and Fiverr have radically transformed the nature of art and design work. Those who specialize in graphic arts, painting, illustration, photography, and clothing and jewelry design can find paying customers using these apps; however, Fiverr and Upwork keep 20 percent of each transaction, which means an artist charging $1,000 for a painting only receives $800. Those who do not wish to pay these costs can promote their gigs for free on Instagram and other social media sites.

Keepsake Jewelry

Aziza Browne is a creative individual who taps her artistic inspirations to power a profitable side gig. Browne, who was born in 2003, began making jewelry as a child. From the

Jewelry designers, photographers, illustrators, and other artists can find paying customers through various apps or by featuring their work on social media sites. Some also turn to sites designed to help crafters sell their work.

time she was young, Browne's friends and family members were eager to purchase her earrings and other pieces. During her college years in New York City, Browne took courses in glass bead making, metalsmithing, and jewelry design offered by local art studios. After college, Browne took a full-time job at the Museum of Modern Art (MoMA) in New York City but decided to launch a jewelry-making side gig she calls Aziza Jewelry. While her MoMA paycheck covered her living expenses, she was able to improve her business prospects by taking advantage of various locally offered grants and scholarships. The New York Foundation for the Arts provides low-income artists with free classes in business development, social media marketing, and search engine optimization (having a site come up closer to the top of an online search). Similar classes are offered by arts councils in cities throughout the country. Browne was able to purchase a new laptop after receiving a grant from the Up & Running Grant Program offered by eBay. Those who receive the grant also enjoy free access to eBay's Seller School, which provides training and coaching by expert sellers. Browne picks up the story: "Eventually, I began selling my jewelry online and was interviewed on a local TV news station for a show called the *Working Woman's Report* and I began to receive other valuable press in magazines and online blog posts, which helped me gain exposure and loyal customers that continue to purchase from me year after year."[18]

In 2020 Browne was making around $5,000 a month and was no longer working at MoMA. She attributed her success to her unique product line. Browne makes mother/daughter matching earring sets to order. And her keepsake word necklaces, which spell out words, are popular especially with those who have interesting or unusual names. Browne attracts customers on Instagram, Facebook, and YouTube and sells her pieces on Amazon, eBay, and Etsy. She keeps in touch with customers through an email newsletter while blogging about her gig for *HuffPost* and small design publications.

Browne recommends that solo entrepreneurs join peer-to-peer mentoring groups, called mastermind groups. "Through these groups, I have . . . found out about opportunities to take free classes and receive scholarships," she reports, adding, "and you can find out about opportunities that are not available to the general public by joining specialized groups in your field and through organization memberships in your field."[19]

Dyeing to Expand a Side Gig

Like Browne, Jake Kenyon found side-gig success by filling an artistic niche that was ignored by others. Kenyon was twenty-nine years old in 2020 when he contracted a mild case of COVID-19. During his recovery he was forced to take time off from his job as a speech pathologist at a hospital in Providence, Rhode Island. Before he got sick, Kenyon spent his spare time hand-dyeing yarn. He created a rainbow of unique colors with notable names like Astral Ascent and Venus Fly Trap, which he marketed under the name Kenyarn on his personal website and on Shopify. In 2019 Kenyon brought in about $20,000 from his side gig.

Like many people, Kenyon reassessed his life choices during the pandemic and decided working on Kenyarn made him happier than his day job. As it happened, Kenyon's timing was good: the pandemic drove many people to take up knitting and crocheting as a way to relax and pass the time. Kenyon promoted his business on Instagram with folksy posts that described his artistic inspirations. In 2020 Kenyon's gross sales jumped to $125,000, and after quitting his job in early 2021, he was on track to earn $200,000.

Some people find that they prefer their side gigs to their regular jobs. And sometimes they even earn enough money to live on. This is what happened to one person who developed a following for his hand-dyed yarns.

Side-Hustle Success on Instagram

Experts say the first step to launching a side hustle on Instagram is to start with an interesting product that can be clearly defined on social media. In a few short sentences you should be able to explain what your product is, why it is unique, and why your audience would love it. Instagram is a visual medium, and you can make your product pop off the screen with a good branding campaign. This involves producing an eye-catching logo, catchphrases, and hashtags. Promote your product several times a week with content that includes photos, memorable quotes, short tutorials, behind-the-scenes videos, and other clickable content.

Once these steps are completed, you can grow your following by promoting your account to friends and family members and asking them to do the same. Tap into your target audience by joining existing communities where your product would be well received. Once your Instagram side hustle is up and running, learn to track your success with analytic tools like Instagram Insights. This will help you see which of your posts received the most engagements, shares, and likes. After taking all these steps, you might see your side hustle start to take off.

Kenyon says that creating his side gig was not easy and offers this advice: "If you're not willing to put in the hours, don't expect to make a ton of money off your side hustle. When I started Kenyarn, I was dyeing yarn in my kitchen every Tuesday and Saturday—the days I wasn't on shift at the hospital. . . . During work lunches, I sat in my car updating the website with new photos and product listings from my phone."[20]

Kenyon constantly experiments with colors and new techniques, such as tie-dyeing; this helps set him apart from his competition. While creating remarkable yarns, Kenyon interacts with prospective customers on Ravelry.com, a social networking site that its users call the Facebook for knitters. He also connects with his seventeen thousand Instagram followers by posting three to four times a week. He says this has played a major role in boosting his business. Kenyon offers this advice to others who hope to start a successful side gig: "I often share Instagram Stories and posts giving people a behind-the-scenes look at my dyeing process. I'm very transparent about what it's like to run my own business—the successes and challenges, and even my flaws. Your voice should always be authentic. Customers want to know where their money is going and what the person behind the brand stands for."[21]

An Artistic Success

Kenyon's success shows the importance of clearly defining one's product, understanding one's target audience, and creating an appealing personal brand. Painter Isaac Pelayo also followed these steps to launch a successful side gig.

Pelayo was just two years old in 1999 when his father handed him a marking pen and told him to draw something. By the time he was eleven the Los Angeles resident was winning art contests at school. By age twenty Pelayo had taught himself to paint and was talented enough to land many an artist's dream job—painting animations at Disney. Then the pandemic struck. Pelayo was laid off and forced to move into his father's one-bedroom apartment. He says he didn't expect to be called back to work and suffered through a period of stress and uncertainty. With nothing much to do during the lockdown, Pelayo set up an easel and began painting every day.

Pelayo had no art agent or art gallery support, but he is a skilled oil painter with a talent for re-creating paintings by European masters such as Leonardo da Vinci and Rembrandt. But he added his own thoroughly modern twist—what he calls Street Baroque. This style melds classic art themes with graffiti art and celebrity portraits. As renowned artist Shepard Fairey explains, "Isaac Pelayo knows how to capture the essence of a subject, but is not afraid to take liberties to tweak that essence and add his own narrative."[22]

Pelayo's unusual paintings garnered attention when he posted photos of them on Instagram. In 2020 his Instagram following grew to over one hundred thousand, and some of his followers became customers. The rapper and fellow entrepreneur Diddy commissioned Pelayo to paint a portrait of the deceased rap mogul Biggie in the style of a Rembrandt painting. The rapper Westside Gunn purchased twenty paintings averaging $15,000 each after seeing Pelayo's Instagram posts. Some of these paintings Gunn used on his album covers. Other customers include NASCAR driver Jeff Hamilton and NFL defensive tackle D.J. Reader. Pelayo is also a licensed tattoo artist who has inked notables such as TikTok star Jaden Hossler.

Pelayo sold more than fifty paintings in 2020 and made well over $100,000. He set up an art studio in the garage of a house he bought for cash in Los Angeles. Pelayo continues to promote his art hustle on Instagram. He spends time curating his feed and studying how to fine-tune his algorithms to grow his customer base. Sometimes he pays Instagram for promotions to help expand his audience. He is also working with TikTok creators to attract more clicks and clients. Pelayo doubts he will ever go back to Disney. "It's been a long journey," Pelayo said in 2021. "But you know, I think it's paying off."[23]

Work Hard and Believe in Yourself

Most designers and artists do not find instant Instagram success, but those who can create eye-catching posts while promoting their work on other social media sites can build a clientele. Most who do end up with successful side gigs start small and work hard. And there is no barrier to entry. Artists do not need agents or managers, and they do not have to please editors or bosses who do not understand them. They only need a good product, a flair for sales, and a belief in their product and in themselves.

Chapter Four

Writing and Translating

Side Gig Stats

73 percent of digital content side hustlers such as bloggers, podcasters, and video makers say they plan to quit their day jobs at some point to become full-time creators.

"Infographic: The State of the Side Hustle," Podia Labs, 2021. www.podia.com.

Almost everybody is a writer. Some only tap out texts or short posts to social media. Others maintain blogs and personal websites filled with pages of writing. But of all the billions of people who type away every day on phones and keyboards only a small percentage get paid for what they write. According to the US Bureau of Labor Statistics (BLS), about seventy-nine thousand people were working as self-employed writers in 2019. This group ranges from best-selling authors to those who run side hustles writing ad copy, listicles, email blasts, instruction manuals, website content, press releases, and blogs. Side-hustling authors also work on speeches, legal briefs, grant proposals, podcasts, and video, film, and TV scripts. These writing gigs pay anywhere from $10 to $180 an hour. Oftentimes, writers work with freelance editors who assign gigs and check facts, spelling, grammar, and punctuation. Sometimes copy is rewritten in other languages by side-gigging translators.

Students with Writing Side Gigs

While many side gigs require workers to be at least eighteen years old, there is no minimum age for writers. There are countless blogs on the web written by kids as young as seven, who express their ideas about art, music, movies, sports, and school. While these blogs rarely earn money, blogging improves a person's writing skills. Blogs also generate links, likes, and hashtags that can be used later in a portfolio to land side gigs.

Sometimes teens, and even younger kids, get their writing published in newspapers and magazines. *Sports Illustrated Kids* hires ten talented students from across the country every year for its Kid Reporters! program. In 2020, the online magazine published articles about tennis, baseball, basketball, and other sports written by young reporters, including eleven-year-old Cole Dunchick, thirteen-year-old Emma Abramson, and fourteen-year-old Anna Laible. These full-time students were all paid for their work.

Almost any teen with writing skills can start a successful side hustle if they are willing to commit to the task. Rainier Harris was a fifteen-year-old high schooler in New York City in 2019 when he turned his passion for writing into a moneymaking side gig. While Harris initially set his sights on writing for national publications, he knew he needed to build a portfolio first. He describes his strategy: "I read my local and regional newspapers, looked for where they could use some extra coverage, and figured out how I could fill in that gap. I wrote about everything from video games to food, to local politics, to subways, to sewage floods for publications like the *Queens Eagle*, *Bushwick Daily*, and *City Limits*."[24]

Harris gained experience at neighborhood newspapers, and got paid for it, while conducting research to land bigger gigs. He read articles about the journalism profession and watched YouTube videos made by aspiring young writers. Harris says one of his most valuable resources was the *Writer's Co-Op* podcast by journalists Wudan Yan and Jenni Gritters. Several episodes covered the importance of networking, or making connections, with editors who are in charge of hiring writers. As Harris explains: "What it really came down to was sending a short, two-paragraph email to the editors at my favorite publications, introducing myself and asking if they were available for a quick call or Zoom meeting. . . . I made sure to include links to my website, portfolio, and samples of my writing."[25]

Harris was happily surprised when nine out of twelve editors he contacted responded to his emails. He held meetings, pitched his ideas, and explained to editors how their publication could benefit from his writing. Harris's presentations were clear and well rehearsed. He stuck to the points he wanted to make, and when the call ended he thanked the editors for their time. He followed up by sending interested editors full-length pitches. "I may not land every pitch I send, but the connection is still there," Harris writes. "As I kept sending fine-tuned pitches, even if they were

The proliferation of online blogs has been a boon to teens and adults who want to develop side gigs that involve writing. These side gigs can turn into other writing opportunities and, sometimes, full-time careers.

Strange Side Gigs for Writers

Side-gigging writers most often focus on creating blogs, ad copy, e-books, and website content. But there are hundreds of weird writing gigs available to those who are willing to write whatever the market demands. One popular writing niche involves romance and lost love. Lauren Spear, founder of LittleZotz Writing, has written love letters, breakup letters, and dating profiles for clients willing to pay from $5 to $25. For an experienced writer like Spear, such letters can take less than fifteen minutes to compose.

Sometimes writers are hired to keep romance alive. Dan Virgillito, who usually focuses on business-to-business (B2B) content, once had a gig writing personal emails to the wife of a busy business leader. Virgillito says the businessman "was often away and wanted to make her feel closer by sharing something that happened to him, telling stories and reminding her about previous experiences they shared." Virgillito earned $300 per email for this work. While some might be unwilling to write love letters or personal emails, there is money to be made from writing weird copy that only a few people will ever see.

Quoted in Sophie Lizard, "Weird Writing Assignments: These Writing Gigs Pay Up to $800/Each," The Penny Hoarder, August 9, 2019. www.thepennyhoarder.com.

rejected, my editors became more accustomed to what I liked to pitch and what I tend to write about. Some started to commission me for future assignments related to that topic."[26]

Harris was successful. By the time he was sixteen his articles had appeared in the *New York Times*, *Business Insider*, and other national publications. While he focuses on maintaining his grades, Harris manages to write about two stories a month. And his side gig brought in about $10,000 in 2020. Harris keeps track of his pitches, invoices, and deadlines using a Google spreadsheet. He offers this advice to other young writers: "I'm still a teenager, and I know that not every editor may take me seriously. But my belief in myself has gotten me this far, and I know that through hard work, I am capable of achieving my dreams."[27]

Translating Words into Money

Almost every newspaper and magazine publishes editions in Spanish, Mandarin Chinese, French, and other languages. These publications provide gigs to those who have the skills to translate words written by others. And according to the BLS, the demand for translators is expected to grow by 20 percent through 2029, much faster than the 4 percent average for all occupations.

If you can read and write in more than one language, translation is a great side gig that can grow into a full-time career. Jennifer Thomé was born in Germany and grew up speaking German and English. When she was twenty she spent a year in China, where she learned the language enough to land a job translating nameplates on government buildings from Chinese into English. In 2020 Thomé had numerous gigs she called language hustles: "Once you get into the field, you'll be overwhelmed by how many ways there are to earn money with your second language. There is transcription (creating a transcript of an audio or video), subtitling, interpretation, social media management, writer, editor, virtual assistant and personal assistant work, and more."[28]

Thomé has no science background but has translated physics papers. Although she is not a marketer, she has translated social media campaigns. She has also translated medical information for individual patients. Thomé believes anyone with an intermediate skill level in another language can successfully perform these kinds of gigs: "None of these things were in my area of expertise . . . but if you're willing to learn and put in the effort and are detail-oriented and a good communicator, people will keep on sending you work."[29]

Translators only need a computer and an internet connection to get started. A microphone and a good camera can come in handy for those who are working with social media or e-commerce clients. A translator who wishes to work in a specialty field such as legal or medical translation might be required to obtain certification, which is offered by the American Translators Association. Newbies can promote their services on social media sites. Niche networking sites like TranslatorsCafé are useful to those hoping to connect with clients and colleagues.

While there is a learning curve for those who wish to translate as a side gig, those who take the initiative find that there is a huge

Fluency in two or more languages can be transformed into side gigs that provide translation services. Some translators are even earning decent money doing voice-overs for commercials.

demand for their services in the $46 billion translation industry. Writing in 2020, Thomé states, "Long story short, everything that happens in English also happens in other languages, and if you can find companies who have it happening in multiple languages, you've found yourself a customer. Tech startups, medical companies, insurance companies, book publishers, law firms, translation firms. . . . These are just a list of the types of companies I have worked for this year."[30]

Thomé says translators earn an average of $25 an hour, but as an experienced translator she can charge $40 an hour. She also earns income from her educational website, Turnkey Translator. Translators who do voice-overs for commercials can earn hundreds of dollars a day. And side-hustler translators have an edge over others when entering the workforce. Companies are eager to hire workers who understand multiple languages. Beyond money, translation work can be very satisfying, as Thomé notes: "On a 'big picture' level we help build the bridges between people, cultures, and companies."[31]

By building bridges, translators and writers can earn extra money, gain confidence, and make their lives a little bit better. Catherine Baab-Muguira says it best when she explains that her writing side gig provides relief from the day-to-day boredom of her marketing job: "The side hustle [is] . . . a hedge against feeling stuck and dull."[32] She calls her side gig the "luxury of writing." That might be the perfect term for a side hustle that is personally satisfying while helping pay the bills.

Chapter Five

Music and Video

As most professional musicians know, the music business is tough and competitive. Even the biggest stars start at the bottom. And most musicians who occupy the lower rungs of the music industry depend on day jobs to get by. Those who want to ascend to the top must be diligent, clever, and resourceful. The same can be said of those who work in video and animation. While a select few bring in the big bucks shooting videos or creating animated features, most who create cartoons or shoot ads work behind the scenes for low pay and little recognition.

The singer/songwriter Sereda, who performs using only her last name, is familiar with the basic dynamics of the entertainment business. Sereda moved to Los Angeles in 2012 in hopes of becoming the next big singing sensation. She did the things she thought would get her there: she recorded demos, met with agents and record label executives, and played low-paying gigs in bars for the exposure. Nothing seemed to work. She explains: "I was contemplating whether I was going to quit music, because it's a grinding, grueling thing. I came to L.A. with a dream, and I basically failed."[33]

While trying to establish herself as a recording artist, Sereda worked multiple side hustles in and out of the entertainment industry. She delivered meals for Postmates, waitressed in a bar, and landed a few small acting roles. Sereda also wrote jingles and soundtrack songs for advertisements and films, which sometimes brought in $5,000 for a few minutes of music. But Sereda's most lucrative side hustle came from an unexpected venue. A friend introduced her to Twitch, the livestreaming gaming platform that attracts millions of viewers.

Sereda is not a gamer, but she thought her songwriting skills might attract some fans on Twitch. In 2019 she began livestreaming herself on the site while she wrote new songs. By 2021 she had more than two hundred thousand followers and was earning $4,500 a month. "It's drawn an audience of people who love that magical eureka moment when the perfect melody hits the perfect instrumental," Sereda says. "It's like watching an artist paint."[34]

Sereda used her money to build a home studio, and she learned how to professionally record and mix music. She believes her Twitch channel is popular because she is willing to demonstrate the basic fundamentals of writing and recording songs. This is something major artists rarely reveal.

While the money is good, the work is never easy. Sereda writes songs from three to seven hours a day while an average of 750 people watch her every move. Nights are given over to performance; in 2020 Sereda played almost thirty virtual concerts, playing and talking to fans for up to four hours a night. But she is amazed by the success she has found through her unconventional music side gig: "The support that I have received from people who have come to find my channel on Twitch is something I've never experienced," she says. "Here I am, an independent artist with no record label, no publishing deal, no manager, no help from anybody, literally just me and this platform, Twitch."[35]

Multimedia Talents

Musicians like Sereda can use their talents to obtain a variety of side gigs. They can contribute to other people's recordings as a session musician or even work as a video game sound designer who creates music and sounds for games. They can also offer online lessons in songwriting or studio production. Some musicians find that their technical studio skills can be useful for finding gigs in video production. They might get work behind the camera, shooting videos for other acts. Some find work as editors who

Musical talent can be a creative outlet and a side gig. Nontraditional venues, such as livestreamed gaming platforms, can connect musicians to a whole new fan base and bring in income at the same time.

assemble raw video footage, dialogue, and sound effects into smooth, finished products ready for broadcasting.

In the world of audiovisual production, YouTube, TikTok, and Instagram might be thought of as crossroads where musicians, photographers, animators, and video editors meet. These sites are filled with visual content, and a lot of it is crude and amateurish. But the video content that attracts the most clicks tends to be well made.

When Jack Cole saw the good and bad on YouTube in 2017, he felt inspired to become a video editor. Cole started his side hustle by learning the nuts and bolts of video editing from YouTube tutorials. After he mastered editing skills, he searched for jobs on freelancing site Upwork. Many ads on the site were posted by social media influencers who wanted to add a professional touch to their videos. Cole soon found himself getting paid for editing down raw video footage into what are called micro-videos. These are one-minute, fast-paced videos that his clients post on Twitter and Instagram. While Cole charged only twenty dollars to do a micro-video, he was able to produce around ten per hour. Cole realized he could make more money from his side gig by starting his own YouTube channel to teach people how to do their own video editing. By 2021 Cole had become a video editing influencer. He had more than 375,000 subscribers and was bringing in thousands of dollars from advertisers who paid him to promote their products.

Telling Jokes with Lego Animation

Andrew Morrey had no professional editing skills when he made his first, amateurish Instagram videos. But Morrey's stop-motion animations that featured LEGO figures acting out silly jokes were entirely unique. Thousands of LEGO lovers soon discovered Morrey's silly videos, which helped him start a successful side gig.

Morrey did not start out to make LEGO animations. He had had a longtime urge to produce a TV sitcom. He wrote a script with a friend but had a big problem: Producing a sitcom costs millions of dollars and requires the skills of dozens of people, includ-

Video Game Sound Designers

Video games would not be very exciting without the music and sounds that enhance the emotional impact of the action. These effects are created by video game sound designers who are often freelance musicians. Sound designers work from a script to break the game down into a number of sections, including locations, environments, characters, weapons, and vehicles. Each one of these elements needs unique music, a voice, ambient sounds, and sound effects. Ted Wennerström is familiar with the process. He is a musician who freelances as a video game composer and sound designer. Wennerström says that when he started out, most of his time was not spent making music but looking for his next job: "emailing, marketing, connecting, emailing some more, doing a Twitter campaign, networking, and so on." He recommends that newbies keep their day jobs to stay afloat and never turn down any game work. Even free jobs can be added to your audio résumé. And as with most successful side hustles, try to find something that makes you stand out from the crowd. "Figure out what you can do that most other composers can't. . . . What makes you unique, only you can know."

Quoted in Jason W. Bay, "My Life as a Video Game Audio Freelancer: What I Wish I Knew Starting Out," Game Industry Career Guide, 2021. www.gameindustrycareerguide.com.

ing actors, lighting technicians, camera operators, and stylists. Then Morrey hit on an idea. He thought, "Maybe I could make it with LEGO animation."[36]

A video that appears to make solid objects—like LEGO figures—move is called stop-motion animation. To create a stop-motion video, animators shoot a single frame of an object, move the object slightly by hand, and shoot another frame. When the single shots run continuously in a video at a certain speed, the object appears to move around the screen with fluid motion. Morrey had little experience creating stop-motion animation, and at first his LEGO characters moved with somewhat jerky motions. But, he says, "the videos were ok, and I was the only person with LEGO animations on Instagram. I would also share these videos on YouTube."[37]

Morrey uploaded his animations to his YouTube channel, CheepJokes. Within six months he was contacted by an advertising company that wanted to pay him for three thirty-second stop-motion videos for Regal Cinemas. The animations, put together into a single video, went on to receive over 7 million hits. But a year passed before Morrey found another paying gig. In the meantime, he built his audience on social media by creating LEGO animation videos that were racking up millions of hits. By 2017 Morrey had found a niche among dedicated LEGO fans. His number of followers spiked after he made promotional animations for Disney films that he linked to his CheepJokes channel. This led Morrey to create a LEGO-lovers website called Brick-Banter, which features photographs, videos, and chat rooms dedicated to the small plastic bricks. Morrey does not make as many animations as he used to because they are time consuming to produce. He spends most of his free time on BrickBanter, editing articles, adding photos, creating thumbnails, and posting to social media.

With the explosive popularity of YouTube, TikTok, and other online platforms, opportunities for video-editing side gigs abound. Skilled video editors can earn money helping clients make high-quality videos.

For all his success, Morrey, who lives in Australia, still had his day job in the financial industry in 2021. Successful side hustles like Morrey's take a lot of time, skill, and luck. "If you start vlogging on YouTube . . . you should be doing it because you enjoy it and because you love creating content and want to share it with the world. If it's good, you might get followers. If you're lucky, you make money."[38]

Morrey's advice could be applied to anyone pursuing side hustles that involve cameras, computers, recording equipment, or musical instruments. Producing share-worthy content that continues to attract followers week after week takes hard work and determination. But if you are doing what makes you happy, your enthusiasm will come through in your content, your goals will be easier to achieve, and you might just make some money.

Chapter Six

Making Instructional Videos

Side Gig Stats

Over 33 percent of side hustlers earn $500 or more per month from their gigs.

Megan Robinson, "Survey: 1 in 4 Side Hustlers Need the Extra Money to Make Ends Meet," Dollarsprout, July 22, 2021. https://dollarsprout.com.

Every day, millions of people visit YouTube when they need expert advice to solve a problem. The site contains a vast wealth of human knowledge, with videos that cover everything from how to make pasta to how to install plumbing. If you want to knit a scarf, learn to play the tuba, or even launch a tutorial side hustle, you can be sure someone has uploaded a video on the subject.

Creators of popular tutorials can branch out into other successful side hustles. They might offer one-on-one lessons online or create websites that feature entire courses on a subject. Those who have a YouTube channel can participate in the site's AdSense program, which tallies every click on each video. While figures vary, AdSense generally pays an average of eighteen cents per video view, or eighteen dollars per thousand. Google, which owns YouTube, keeps 32 percent, so a poster might only earn a little over twelve dollars for every thousand views. While that does not sound like much, tutorial posters who attract hundreds of thousands of subscribers can turn their side hustles into full-time gigs.

Teaching English

Some successful tutorial side giggers are trained teachers. Gabby Wallace is an American with a degree in education who has taught English as a second language (ESL) in Japan. While in Japan, Wallace created a few short videos to help her students, which she posted to YouTube. She later moved back to the United States to work at a university but continued to make and post short videos for her former students. Soon, however, Wallace noticed that people who were not her students were also finding her videos online, thanks to Google and YouTube search engines. After six months, Wallace got a message from YouTube asking her whether she wanted to earn money from her videos. "It was almost an accidental business that I created," Wallace says. "No funding, no investors, no business plan. I just wanted to help my students. . . . I didn't even know how to edit. . . . It's really embarrassing, but you can do this even with very little training."[39]

Before long, Wallace began receiving requests from students who wanted her to teach them on Skype. These gigs brought in about $100 a week, and the requests kept coming. Wallace's "Go Natural English" channel on YouTube soon had ten thousand subscribers and was bringing in around $250 a month. While keeping her full-time teaching job, Wallace decided to grow her business. She created a video course for paid subscribers that features lessons, quizzes, and exclusive content. Within a year she had a hundred thousand subscribers and was making good money. By 2021 her YouTube channel was thriving, with around 1.9 million subscribers in 130 countries. And Wallace was earning around $120,000 a year from her downloadable courses, sponsorships, and AdSense revenue.

Wallace credits her success to various lessons she learned along the way. She says she always asks for viewer feedback so she can improve her content. For example, she began incorporating pop culture subjects into her lessons to make them more relevant to her audience. Wallace also learned how to shoot and edit high-quality videos that engage viewers and prompt users to share. She was able to make more money from her content by taking on sponsorships; that is to say, companies pay Wallace to use their products and services in her videos. And she uses her YouTube videos to drive viewers to her website where they can purchase her course in video and e-book formats.

Wallace says it is important to stay relevant on YouTube. She does this by posting around three videos a week to keep viewers coming back for more. While this requires hours of work, Wallace says her experience has been emotionally rewarding: "Honestly, [people] benefit so much from collaborating, whether it's simply sharing each other's links, doing a collaborative video or interviewing each other on a podcast [has] been just a huge source of not only income—but growing our respective communities."[40]

The Successful Slime Queen

Whereas Wallace is a trained professional, finding success with tutorial videos does not necessarily require a college degree. Sometimes all it takes is craft, creativity, and good timing. Karina Garcia turned those elements into a successful side hustle that garnered her the title of Slime Queen of the Internet. And Garcia knows slime; not the stuff that oozes down the bathtub drain but the colorful, sticky toy slime that millions of kids play with every day.

The viscous substance known as slime has been sold by toy companies for decades and has been featured on Nickelodeon shows and in films like *Ghostbusters*. While the popularity of slime has gone up and down over the years, its popularity exploded in

the late 2010s. And Garcia was one of the driving forces behind the slime craze.

Before Garcia rose to prominence as the Slime Queen, she only saw slime on the dirty plates she handled as a waitress. She was living with her parents and five siblings in two house trailers in Southern California. But Garcia says she was always an arts-and-crafts type of kid who made her own beauty supplies. With her twin sister's encouragement, Garcia made her first YouTube video, "Easy DIY Lipsticks!" The video received a few hundred hits, which inspired Garcia to make more do-it-yourself (DIY) makeup tutorials. She branched out to include videos aimed at kids, such as making DIY fudgesicles and thumb-drive decorations. While looking for new projects, Garcia got the idea for slime. "I decided to do sensory play, like squishy things because I feel that's what kids like. They're into Play-Doh and anything else squishy,"[41] she explains.

Garcia found a basic slime recipe on Pinterest consisting of Elmer's Glue, water, and borax (a laundry product). "This was the most basic slime ever," Garcia says, "[so] I started throwing random stuff in it to make different textures."[42] Garcia continued to waitress but spent her spare time creating innovative slime tutorials. She showed viewers how to mix basic slime ingredients with dyes, soaps, glitter, and other substances that would make the goo stretchy, fluffy, or crackly. Each video had an impossible-to-ignore thumbnail, a small, colorful video that often featured Garcia laughing, making funny faces, and generally acting goofy.

Buying a House with Slime

Garcia's focus on slime started attracting enough clicks, likes, and subscriptions to bring in some extra spending cash. Her first check from YouTube was only $50, but soon she was regularly getting checks as large as $10,000. Within a few years, the Karina Garcia YouTube channel had more than two hundred videos with recipes for things like slime balloons, slime bubblegum, and spicy ramen slime. The videos were attracting millions of hits; her 2016 video "100 Pounds of Slime" was viewed more than 17 million times. Garcia's tutorials were so popular that they even raised Elmer's Glue sales by 25 percent and spawned a temporary glue shortage.

By 2021 Garcia's YouTube channel had over 9 million subscribers, and her videos had racked up more than 1.6 billion views. The Slime Queen also attracted sponsorship deals and corporate advertising and was earning over $200,000 a month. Garcia, who quit her job as a waitress, bought a large house for her family in Riverside, California, with a swimming pool, hot tub, and game room. She jokes that she is the only person who ever bought a house with slime but that she also feels blessed: "It's really important to take care of my family," Garcia says. "Because we grew up not having much."[43]

Succeeding Against the Odds

While some tutorial creators find success on YouTube, it can take a long time to earn money with a side gig that revolves around making educational videos. YouTube figures show that it takes an average of six months to gain one hundred subscribers to a channel. But a channel must have at least one thousand subscribers, and accrue four thousand hours of watch time over the course of twelve months, to earn money through YouTube's AdSense program. Nine out of ten channels never manage to attract five thousand subscribers. Since it takes an average of a hundred thousand views to attract a thousand subscribers, channels with low numbers never earn a profit. And the competition for subscribers is fierce. Five hundred hours of video footage is uploaded to YouTube every minute of every day. While the odds of success are not great for tutorial creators, those who generate enough traffic to participate in AdSense can still maintain a good side hustle. A 2018 study by German science professor Mathias Bärtl showed that 97 percent of YouTube creators who participated in AdSense earned around $12,140 annually.

Garcia might be one of the most successful tutorial creators on social media, but there is an eager audience for all kinds of DIY videos. Around half of US adults say they have visited YouTube to learn how do to something they had never done before, according to the Pew Research Center. And hundreds of tutorial videos are uploaded every day by side hustlers hoping to make a few bucks sharing their knowledge with others. While most tutorial creators will never earn enough to quit their jobs, those who attract thousands of subscribers can earn enough to at least pay off some bills. For some, like Garcia, however, a side gig can lead to so much more. As Garcia puts it, "I feel like I have exceeded my expectations and never thought this was really possible."[44]

Chapter Seven

Technology and Programming

Side Gig Stats

About one third of millennials from ages 18 to 26 were working on a side gig in 2020, and 66 percent of them performed their gig at least once a week.

Bill Acholla, "23 Side Hustle Statistics You Need to Know for 2021," Bill Acholla Marketing Tips, October 24, 2020. www.billacholla.com.

The 2020 COVID-19 pandemic changed many things, including the English language. New buzzwords, such as social distancing, lockdown, and self-isolation quickly entered daily conversations. Another new pandemic-related term, *digital nomad*, came into use to describe laid-off tech workers who discovered a new kind of freedom when they did not have to go into the office every day. These tech workers, who could perform their jobs anywhere there was an internet connection, used their skills to launch side gigs. Some left expensive tech hubs like San Francisco and New York City to work from rural America or even tourist destinations like Hawaii. Other digital nomads took on tech side gigs while traveling.

Many people went back to work in 2021, but digital nomads remained in high demand as tech companies increased their hiring of part-time and temporary tech experts. Side-gigging software developers, game designers, cybersecurity specialists, website builders, and other information technology (IT) professionals found they could work as much, or as little, as they wanted. And most tech side hustlers were still pulling in anywhere from $40 to $75 an hour, according to Upwork.

Figures from the Computing Technology Industry Association (CompTIA) explain why the job market is so hot for digital nomads. The $5 trillion tech industry is expected to grow by 25 percent by 2025, but there is a shortage of high-tech expertise in many industries. This leaves companies competing for talent on freelance technology job websites like Braintrust, Catalant, and Toptal. As Joseph Fuller, professor of management practice at Harvard, explains: "These gig platforms screen freelancers . . . and [publish] ratings from their former employers. That creates the equivalent of an online talent supermarket."[45]

A Self-Taught Website Designer

Charvee Buch is someone who benefited from the online talent platform known as Fiverr. When the pandemic hit, the thirty-year-old Buch was running Wellnus Company, a business that sold organic, biodegradable cleaning wipes online. While the demand for cleaning wipes skyrocketed, Buch's product did not meet government guidelines for sanitizing wipes because they did not contain germ-killing alcohol.

As the number of Wellnus orders dropped rapidly, Buch put her tech skills to work to start a side gig. She drew on the web-building experience she had gained from creating the Wellnus website. She explains: "I spent six months just researching, researching, researching. I figured out everything to do with designing a website."[46] Buch learned to incorporate creativity, coding skills, and business acumen with graphics, photos, sounds, and other features. When it was finished, the Wellnus website was eye-catching, functional, and secure.

When her main business slowed, Buch was inspired to use her newly developed talents to pursue a side gig as a web designer. She offered her services on Fiverr and landed her first client within two days. From there her web design business grew rapidly. Buch attributes her success to the stress the pandemic put on small businesses; many were forced to swiftly improve their websites or create new ones to reach customers stuck at home. Buch was soon earning over $1,000 a month. "I was very surprised," she says. "From a person who has no experience within that field, I did not expect anything."[47]

Some website designers on Fiverr charge up to $1,200 for full website construction. While she sets higher rates for successful companies, she offers rates as low as $150 to small, struggling businesses. Buch's websites, which are attractive and easy to use, draw in clients from a wide range of industries, including medicine, fashion, and beauty. And her clients live all over the world: "I've had orders from Australia . . . India and New Zealand. So it's been really interesting to see my clientele from these different countries, and you can see that same trend of them scrambling to try and get online."[48]

With her Wellnus Company experience, Buch is able to provide more than website design services to her stressed-out clients. She offers free tips about marketing online, building a presence on social media, and efficiently shipping products to customers. Buch says she does this because it is important for her "to provide empathy and . . . the tools to be successful."[49] Extending goodwill to customers is a winning strategy for the self-taught web designer. And the clients whom she helps succeed are sure to return again as customers as their businesses grow.

Offering Compassionate Tech Support

Few people would associate empathy with tech support, but Joel Barker is working to bring kindness and understanding to a field long associated with snooty know-it-alls. Barker is familiar with the confusion and frustration experienced by someone trying to

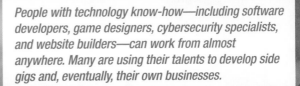

People with technology know-how—including software developers, game designers, cybersecurity specialists, and website builders—can work from almost anywhere. Many are using their talents to develop side gigs and, eventually, their own businesses.

overcome technological hurdles. As the chief strategy officer for a large children's mental health clinic in Minnesota, Barker has seen his coworkers struggle to use a new software program or printer network. Barker's day job also brings him into contact with nonprofit organizations and charities that lack the money to hire IT support staff. So he created Brave North Technology to provide affordable, compassionate tech support for less-than-tech-savvy nonprofits and small businesses.

Barker's original investment of $1,500 was spent setting up a website, registering as a business in Minnesota, and creating marketing materials. The company earned a $3,000 check with its first gig, and this money was reinvested in the business. Barker also signed up investors, using his networking skills to develop relationships. He says he never turned down a meeting with any-one. By 2020, Brave North Technology was earning an annual profit of $90,000.

Cory Althoff: Digital Nomad

Cory Althoff is a self-taught computer wiz who is truly a digital nomad. Althoff graduated from college with a political science degree. He says his degree was not useful for finding a job. He went online and learned the popular programming language Python, which is known to be easier for beginners. Althoff developed his programming skills to the point where he landed a job as a software engineer at eBay in Palo Alto, California.

Later, Althoff took some time off work to backpack through Southeast Asia. He ended up in Bali, a famed resort island in Indonesia, where he had some down time. He started a side hustle as a computer programmer by signing up on the freelance websites Fiverr and Toptal. The money came pouring in, which allowed him to quit his job at eBay. He explains: "As a freelance programmer, you can earn a high income while working from anywhere. Thanks to freelancing, I've been able to visit twenty-six countries on six continents. So far, I've been to North America, South America, Africa, Europe, Australia, and Asia. I'm hoping to add Antarctica to the list soon! Working from a cafe in Tokyo or by the beach doesn't quite feel like work!"

Cory Althoff, "The Successful Freelance Programmer: A Guide to Freelance Programming," *Self-Taught*, 2021. https://selftaught.blog.

Barker does not run Brave North alone. He launched the company with his college friend Brian Roemon, who has IT expertise. The company also hires other experienced IT professionals who set up hardware, teach clients to use software, and install technology related to security and cloud computing. According to the company website, all Brave North workers are trained to bring "empathy, patience, intelligence, active listening, persistence, and positivity"[50] to the job.

Working full-time and maintaining Brave North Technologies as a side gig was not enough for Barker. In 2020 he founded his second side hustle, Great River Strategies, to help grassroots organizations with tasks such as digital marketing, social media management, writing grant applications, and launching corporate partnership programs. Great River Strategies focuses on non-profits in a variety of sectors, including education, health care, disability services, and the environment. Barker says he loves the challenges posed by running two side hustles, both of which allow him to do something he loves while helping make the world a better place.

Technology is becoming more complex every day, and companies are clamoring for experts in blockchain technology, cloud engineering, cybersecurity, data science, and other high-tech fields. This is leading to an increase in the number of digital side gigs for those with degrees and/or expertise in computer engineering, software engineering, information systems, and other tech. At the same time, companies like Google, Apple, Facebook, and Amazon have shown a much greater willingness to work with side-hustling digital nomads. And the change is not only occurring at the biggest tech companies. Many smaller businesses are finding that they can save time and money by hiring side giggers who are up-to-date on the latest technologies. While gig work is not as secure or steady as full-time employment, those who can offer on-demand skills can expect to earn a premium price for their talents.

Source Notes

Introduction: The Growing Side-Gig Economy

1. Quoted in Jennifer Barrett, "Side Hustles Are Helping Many Close the Income Gap in the Pandemic—Here's What to Look For," *Forbes*, October 20, 2020. www.forbes.com.
2. Quoted in Barrett, "Side Hustles Are Helping Many Close the Income Gap in the Pandemic."
3. Quoted in Kim Mackrael, "In the Covid Economy, Laid-Off Employees Become New Entrepreneurs," *Wall Street Journal*, November 18, 2020. www.wsj.com.
4. Kian Bakhtiari, "Generation Side Hustle Is Changing the Face of Marketing," *Forbes*, September 25, 2019. www.forbes.com.
5. Quoted in Barrett, "Side Hustles Are Helping Many Close the Income Gap in the Pandemic."

Chapter One: Little Experience Required

6. Black Sugar Ice Jelly, "What Is It Like to Work for DoorDash," Quora, February 17, 2021. www.quora.com.
7. Quoted in Patricia Escárcega, "The Lives of Essential Workers, One Year into the Pandemic," *Bon Appétit*, February 16, 2021. www.bonappetit.com.
8. Choncé Maddox, "My Honest Review of Being a DoorDash Delivery Driver," The Work at Home Woman, November 26, 2019. www.theworkathomewoman.com.
9. LynneP1978, "Out of Curiosity . . . How Much Do Y'all Usually Make in a Week? Month?," Reddit, 2019. www.reddit.com/r/WagWalker.
10. Baxter, "Auto Detailing Uniforms: 3 Benefits and Where to Buy," Carwash Country, 2021. www.carwashcountry.com.

Chapter Two: Focus on Food

11. Quoted in Alex Williams, "Can You Really Turn a Hobby Into a Career?," *New York Times*, February 13, 2021. www.nytimes.com.
12. Dan Palmer, "My Accidental Side Hustle: Making Frozen Meals!," Budgets are Sexy, July 3, 2019. www.budgetsaresexy.com.
13. Quoted in Hannah Kueck, "Frosting on the Side," *Como*, September 25, 2020. https://comomag.com.

14. Quoted in Kueck, "Frosting on the Side."
15. Quoted in Natalia Guerevich, "After Growing Up Daring His Brother To 'Eat Hotter Stuff,' He's Building a Hot Sauce Empire," *Los Angeles Times*, June 26, 2021. www.latimes.com.
16. Taylor Lorenz, "TikTok, the Fastest Way on Earth to Become a Food Star," *New York Times*, May 24, 2021. www.nytimes.com.
17. Quoted in Lorenz, "TikTok, the Fastest Way on Earth to Become a Food Star."

Chapter Three: Art and Design

18. Quoted in Pat Walls, "How I Started a $5K/Month Side Hustle Selling Custom Word Necklaces," Starter Story, March 12, 2020. www.starterstory.com.
19. Quoted in Walls, "How I Started a $5K/Month Side Hustle Selling Custom Word Necklaces."
20. Jake Kenyon, "This 30-Year-Old Quit His Job to Work on His Side Hustle. Now He's on Track to Make $200,000 in Sales This Year," CNBC, July 13, 2021. www.cnbc.com.
21. Kenyon, "This 30-Year-Old Quit His Job to Work on His Side Hustle."
22. Quoted in Dominic-Madori Davis, "A 24-Year-Old Who Got Laid Off from Disney Turned His Art Side Hustle Into a 6-figure Income and Is Doing Business Almost Entirely on Instagram," Business Insider, March 24, 2021. www.businessinsider.com.
23. Quoted in Davis, "A 24-year-Old Who Got Laid Off From Disney Turned His Art Side Hustle Into a 6-figure Income and Is Doing Business Almost Entirely on Instagram."

Chapter Four: Writing and Translating

24. Rainier Harris, "Teen Who Made $10,000 in a Year at His First Side Hustle: Here's How I Got Successful Fast," Grow Acorns, October 20, 2020. https://grow.acorns.com.
25. Harris, "Teen Who Made $10,000 in a Year at His First Side Hustle."
26. Harris, "Teen Who Made $10,000 in a Year at His First Side Hustle."
27. Harris, "Teen Who Made $10,000 in a Year at His First Side Hustle."
28. Quoted in Caitlin Pyle, "How to Become a Translator: Expert Interview with Jennifer Thomé," Work-at-Home School, 2021. https://workathomeschool.com.
29. Quoted in Pyle, "How to Become a Translator."
30. Quoted in Pyle, "How to Become a Translator."
31. Quoted in Pyle, "How to Become a Translator."
32. Quoted in Atossa Araxia Abrahamian, "The Pain and Joy of the Side Hustle," *Columbia Journalism Review*, Spring/Summer 2018. www.cjr.org.

Chapter Five: Music and Video

33. Quoted in Gili Malinsky, "This Musician Makes $4,500 a Month Streaming Her Songwriting Process on Twitch," CNBC, February 20, 2021. www.cnbc.com.
34. Quoted in Malinsky, "This Musician Makes $4,500 a Month Streaming Her Songwriting Process on Twitch."
35. Quoted in Malinsky, "This Musician Makes $4,500 a Month Streaming Her Songwriting Process on Twitch."
36. Quoted in Christy Laurence, "The Story of a Successful Side-Hustle Told by the Influencer of the Year," Plann, 2021. www.plannthat.com.
37. Quoted in Nishad Kinhikar, "Andrew Morrey—Start Small, Learn as You Go, and Always Keep Improving," Eat My News, June 1, 2021. www.eatmy.news.
38. Quoted in Kinhikar, "Andrew Morrey."

Chapter Six: Making Instructional Videos

39. Quoted in Susan Shain, "This Teacher Used YouTube to Make $120K Last Year—Here's How She Did It," Penny Hoarder, March 5, 2019. www.thepennyhoarder.com.
40. Quoted in Shain, "This Teacher Used YouTube to Make $120K Last Year."
41. Quoted in Claire Martin, "Feel the Noise: Homemade Slime Becomes Big Business," *New York Times*, June 23, 2017. www.nytimes.com.
42. Quoted in Courtney Connley, "This 23-Year-Old Went from Waitressing to Earning Millions as YouTube's 'Slime Queen,'" CNBC, January 30, 2018. www.cnbc.com.
43. Quoted in Connley, "This 23-Year-Old Went from Waitressing to Earning Millions as YouTube's 'Slime Queen.'"
44. Quoted in Connley, "This 23-Year-Old Went from Waitressing to Earning Millions as YouTube's 'Slime Queen.'"

Chapter Seven: Technology and Programming

45. Quoted in Kathy Kristof, "Here's Where Skilled Freelancers Can Find Jobs," *Los Angeles Times*, January 9, 2021. www.latimes.com.
46. Quoted in Tom Huddleston Jr., "This Mom's Fiverr Side-Hustle Earns Her Over $1,000 a Month—and She's Helping Businesses Hurt by Coronavirus," CNBC, June 26, 2020. www.cnbc.com.
47. Quoted in Huddleston, "This Mom's Fiverr Side-Hustle Earns Her Over $1,000 a Month."
48. Quoted in Huddleston, "This Mom's Fiverr Side-Hustle Earns Her Over $1,000 a Month."
49. Quoted in Huddleston, "This Mom's Fiverr Side-Hustle Earns Her Over $1,000 a Month."
50. Brave North Technology, "Our Mission," 2021. www.bravenorthtech.com.

Other Side Gigs Worth Exploring

Arts and crafts instructor
Audiobook production
Brochure design
Cybersecurity expert
Data manager
Diet coach
E-commerce developer
Fortune-teller
Landscape design
Life coach
Logo design
Modeling

Music promotion
Photoshop editing
Podcast writing
Real estate promotion
Search engine optimization
Social media marketing
Sound design
Speechwriting
3-D product animation
Travel writer
Voiceover artist
Web analytics

Editor's note: The US Department of Labor's Bureau of Labor Statistics provides information about hundreds of occupations. The agency's *Occupational Outlook Handbook* describes what these jobs entail, the work environment, education and skill requirements, pay, future outlook, and more. The *Occupational Outlook Handbook* may be accessed online at www.bls.gov/ooh.

Find Out More

Internet Articles

Jennifer Barrett, "Side Hustles Are Helping Many Close the Income Gap in the Pandemic—Here's What to Look For," *Forbes*, October 20, 2020. www.forbes.com.

Baxter, "Auto Detailing Uniforms: 3 Benefits and Where to Buy," Carwash Country, 2021. www.carwashcountry.com.

Kathy Kristof, "Six Figures from Freelancing? This Platform Makes Gig Work Lucrative," *Los Angeles Times*, May 15, 2021. www.latimes.com.

Sangeeta Singh-Kurtz, "This Fashion Brand Took Off During the Pandemic," The Cut, May 20, 2021. www.thecut.com.

Websites

Financial Wolves
https://financialwolves.com
This website features ideas for side hustles, delivery app reviews, online moneymaking ideas, and other information about the gig economy.

Fiverr
https://www.fiverr.com
Fiverr is an online marketplace for freelance services with thousands of listings in dozens of categories. This is the go-to website for anyone wishing to launch a side gig.

Sidehusl
https://sidehusl.com
Award-winning journalist Kathy Kristof runs this site, which has hundreds of ideas for side hustles in various categories that include working, renting, and selling.

Side Hustle School
https://sidehustleschool.com
This site contains hundreds of real-life stories from those who have launched their own successful side hustles; includes audio segments and written transcripts.

Starter Story

www.starterstory.com

Starter Story interviews people who have turned their side hustles into successful businesses. Entrepreneurs are asked how they got started, how they grew their businesses, and what it takes to compete in the field.

Young Adult Money

www.youngadultmoney.com

As the name of this website makes clear, Young Adult Money provides youth-focused information about finding gigs, managing debt, and saving money.

Index

Note: Boldface page numbers indicate illustrations.

Abramson, Emma, 31
Althoff, Cory, 54
American Translators
  Association, 34
animation, 40–42
artist, 28–29

Baab-Muguira, Catherine, 36
Bakhtiari, Kian, 6
Balch, Ashlyn, 18–19
Barker, Joel, 52–55
Bärtl, Mathias, 49
Bernath, Eitan, 20–21
Browne, Aziza, 23–25
Buch, Charvee, 51
Bureau of Labor Statistics (BLS),
  30, 34

car washing/detailing, 13–14
Cole, Jack, 40
Computing Technology Industry
  Association (CompTIA), 51
cook-to-customer apps,
  17–18
Cote, Carol, 15
COVID-19 pandemic, 10
  impact on language, 50

delivery services, 10–11
Diddy, 28
digital nomads, 50–51
DishDivvy (cook-to-customer
  app), 17, 18
dog walker, 11–13, **12**
do-it-yourself (DIY) tutorials,
  47–48
DoorDash, 10
Dunchick, Cole, 31

earnings, 44
  artist, 29
  delivery driver, 11
  dog walker, 11–12, 13
  freelancing tech professional, 51
  self-employed writer, 30
  for tech support, 53
  translator, 35
  from tutorials, 45–46
  web designer, 52
eBay (online auction site), 25
English language tutorials, 45–46
Etsy (website), 5

Facebook, 4, 25, 27, 55
Fairey, Shepard, 28
Financial Wolves (website), 60
Fiverr (website), 5, 9, 23, 60
food freelancers, 17–18, **19**
Freelancers Union, 5
Fuller, Joseph, 51

Garcia, Karina, 46–49
gig economy
  miscellaneous jobs in, 59
  percentage of millennials
    working in, 50
  size of, 5
Girls With Impact, 6
Go Natural English (YouTube
  channel), 45
Google, 33, 45
Gritters, Jenni, 32

Hamilton, Jeff, 29
Hamilton, Steven, 5
Harris, Rainier, 31–33
health insurance, 6–7
health/safety regulations, 8
Hernandez, Andres, 11
Hossler, Jaden, 29

Instagram (photo-sharing site), 6, 27, 28, 40
interviews
  with gig chef, 22
  with side gig driver, 15

jewelry designer, 23–25, **24**

Kenyon, Jake, 25–28

Laible, Anna, 31
letter writing, 33
Lorenz, Taylor, 21

Maddox, Choncé, 11
Morrey, Andrew, 40–43
Musto, Alissa, 6

New York Foundation for the Arts, 24–25

Occupational Outlook Handbook (Bureau of Labor Statistics), 59
opinion polls. *See* surveys

Palmer, Dan, 18
Pelayo, Isaac, 28–29
Pew Research Center, 49
Pham, Thuy, 16
polls. *See* surveys
programmer, 54

Reader, D.J., 29

Sands, Samantha, 4–5
Sereda, 37–38
Sidehusl (website), 60
Side Hustle School (website), 60
sound designer, 41
Spear, Lauren, 33
Sports Illustrated Kids (magazine), 31
Spotify (music streaming site), 37
Starter Story (website), 61
surveys
  on Americans in gig economy, 5

on interest in side gigs, **7**
on percentage of artists/designers self-employed, 23
on percentage of Gen Z expecting to launch businesses, 6

taxes, 6–7
tech support, 52–54
Thomé, Jennifer, 34, 35, 36
TikTok (online platform), 6, 29, 40, 42
  food stars on, 20–21
translators, 33–36
Twitch (music streaming site), 38

Up & Running Grant Program (eBay), 25
Upwork (freelance employment platform), 23, 40, 51

video editor, 40, **42**
video game sound designer, 41
videos, 40–41
  cooking, 20–21
  do-it-yourself (DIY), 47–48
  English language, 45–46
  music instruction, 6
  stop-motion animation, 40–42
Virgillito, Dan, 33

Wallace, Gabby, 45–46
web designer, 51–52
Wennerström, Ted, 41
Westside Gunn, 29
writer, 31–33, **32**
  self-employed, numbers of, 30
Writer's Co-Op (podcast), 32

Yan, Wudan, 32
yarn dyeing, **26**, 26–28
Young Adult Money (website), 61
YouTube (online platform), 20, 44, 45
  educational videos on, 49

Zalkind, Scott, 20

Picture Credits

Cover: Shutterstock